The Vision Book

A Journey into taking Action on your Deepest Desires

Morenike Coker

© 2020 Unapologetically Morenike

TXu 2-232-335

Acknowledgements

I first thank God. I have had a beautiful adventure writing and publishing this book, once again in the beautiful country of Mexico and Diana Vellos Coker.

This book is dedicated to every reader and those who will benefit from taking action in these exercises.

Table of Contents

Acknowledgements 2

How to Read this book: 3

DECLARATION 5

Part One 8

    Getting To Know You 8

    Everything I've Ever Wanted to Have 10

    Things I Want For Others 12

    Craft Your Vision 13

Part Two 14

    Digging Deeper 14

    Inspiring Success 15

    Intentions 16

    Future Journal Entry 17

    Candyman, Candyman! 18

    Resolutions! Resolutions! Resolutions! 19

    Time to Be Of Service to Yourself, Saying Goodbye 21

    Fear in Separation 22

    Calling In Your Soulmates 23

    Soul Tribe Supporters 24

    Soul Tribe/ Wolfpack*: Finish liners 25

    Soul Tribe/Wolfpack: Way-showers 26

    Soul Tribe/ Peers 27

    Core Values 28

Part Three 29

Removing Blockages: Inner Child Work 29

Being a Good Parent to Your Inner Child 30

Resolving Your Past 31

Cartoon time! 32

Part Four 33

Taking Action 33

Getting real! 34

Be Your Own Best Friend Today 36

Failure! 37

Making Space by Clearing the Time 39

Vision Board Time!! 40

Money, Multiple Streams of Income, and Investments 44

Welcome to your vision workbook! Congrats on taking action; you are absolutely going to see rewards. I'm Morenike Coker, and I teach workshops and help others to develop by developing myself. You are getting premium exercises and tips that have helped me to publish my first book, Something to Show For It: Freedom, Faith, and Enlightenment with a One-Way Ticket to Mexico and $200. It also helped me to leave law school after my first year, travel the world and start an e-commerce business and coaching practice with little money. I traveled throughout Southeast Asia starting with $1,500 and a ticket to Bangkok, Thailand, and found myself in five countries including Laos, Cambodia, Vietnam, and Malaysia.

It's the beginning of a new era; we have seen many radical changes happening since the beginning of 2020 via COVID and many have the desire to build something. Using a series of exercises combined with lots of planning, we are going to go through setting up steps in your life to finishing them. We will explore people in your life, remove blockages, learn more steps to move forward and create an amazing life.

Always remember that you are worthy of your dreams and goals. My favorite scripture comes from Romans 12:2 "Do not conform to the pattern of this world, but be transformed by the renewing of your mind." This is a new time that is calling for you to elevate yourself so that the old version of yourself is not coming in the way of the future empire you are building.

I believe in you and all of the amazing things that you have set out to create, all of the generations that will be impacted by your choice to show up and actually, do all of the work.

I'm honored to share these exercises and tips with you. I teach sessions to the general public on the last Monday of every month.

https://unapologeticallymorenike.com/

I am very social, and I would love to meet you there. You can find me on Instagram, YouTube, and Facebook with the name, Unapologetically Morenike.

How to Read this book:

You can jump across different pages or you can go in order. You will find that some of the exercises are built on one another while the others are independent. I recommend taking some time to do this over a specific period (over a three, or six months), depending on what you need to accomplish. Your time is your time; make it a priority to finish this book, no matter how long it takes you. There are several pages left for you to do the activities more than once because as you continue to evolve, your priorities and ideas will shift. Use this like a journal and a calendar.

Can I do this with a friend?

Actually, I recommend it! When I conduct workshops, this is one of the most beneficial tools is sharing because not only are you focusing on something, but the energy and beauty of being supported and supporting others is very powerful and it's playful with the timer. The book of Matthew 18:20 "When two or more are gathered together in my name, I am there."

- I have done these alone, and I found great value in doing them, however, I recommend reading each exercise out loud after it is complete and letting the next person read.

Rule of Sharing:

After each exercise allow the person to speak life into their words and the next person reads. No criticisms, not at all. By sharing you are creating a safe space. And there is life in the power of your tongue. If someone doesn't want to share, honor that. It is encouraged, though.

- I recommend revisiting this often and revising often.

What is this book?

This book is an honest way of sitting down and getting to know yourself and the world around you. It is the first step to building more than what is just in sight. Sight is what is right in front of you; vision encompasses multiple parts of your life and is unconcerned with how it will happen.

What Do I Need?

-A brand new notebook

-YouTube account to watch videos

-Honesty

-An open mind

-Time

-Intention to complete all exercises and apply them.

DECLARATION

Father in the name of Jesus,

I decree and declare that the person reading this will see your transfer of wealth and be prepared for the monumental legacy-building opportunity to express herself/himself that you have prepared especially for them just as you knew every hair on their head.

I decree and declare that this will be a fun journey full of your many promises to give silver instead of stone and gold instead of bronze.

I decree and declare that every energetic, psychological, emotional, spiritual, financial attack, word curse, evil eye, sickness or any type weapon be made impotent and never ever prospers.

I decree and declare that as the reader reviews her/his inspiring story, that whatever was meant for evil, you have worked it out for her/his good and all experiences positive and negative will be made clear for this divine purpose of living life out loud in the freest and happiest way possible.

I decree and declare that all finances and investments continue to increase exponentially and passively and they will know how to advance in this kingdom as first and not last, the head and not the tail.

I decree and declare that the thinking of this reader has expanded and no longer sit in a mentality of someone who works for someone, exchanges money for time, accepts hierarchal relationships, or calls anyone boss *ever* again. The thinking and ideas have expanded from one of greed and survival to she and he who lends to many nations and borrows from none.

I decree and declare that the ideas that come to this reader are ones that come from prosperity, abundance, and knowing the list of passions to live are unending.

I decree and declare that all people who come needing this person's help will go back blessed and abundant.

I decree and declare that as their children's children are benefitting from this work socially, economically, genetically, intellectually; they will have the same spark of desire for you to fulfill their special purpose. I decree and declare that this be a time that while most people are complaining about this pandemic, this reader will use this planning time to grow and will see this as one of the best times of his/her life.

I decree and declare that all of those whom you have assigned to help and level up this reader's life will come out of the woodwork from every direction right as the wrong people are taking their exit.

This is as new season and we have been called and chosen.
Thank you for another day to shine your light on his/her life.
Amen. Amen. And Amen!

Part One

Getting To Know You

These are a series of exercises that are timed to get you to think on your feet and get to know yourself. If you are doing this as a group, it is very entertaining and enlightening. If you are performing it solo, it will raise your vibration.

You are winning!

You will need:
Some Space to do the exercise (café, kitchen table, park, library, group circle etc.)
A timer (phone, stopwatch, etc.)

Everything I Have Ever Wanted to Feel

In crafting your vision, we are going to see where your innermost desires are, when you don't have time to think. You may be very surprised by what comes up. Today, you are going to **set your timer to five minutes**. You are going to write all of the things down that you want to feel.

For example, I want to feel:
in love, the rain on my face, a surfboard under my feet, and the tropical wind of paradise in Mexico.
Dream BIGGER than what you thought was possible.

Revision: Remove the word want and say "I feel" then begin your list.

Everything I've Ever Wanted to Have

In crafting your vision, we are going to see where your innermost desires are when you don't have time to think. You may be very surprised by what comes up. Today, you are going to **set your timer to five minutes.** You are going to write all of the things down that you want to have.

For example, I have three houses in three different countries, have a monkey, new keys to my dream house, etc.

Dream BIGGER than what you thought was possible.

Revision: Remove the word "want" and say "I have" and begin your list. The trick here is writing it as if you already have it.

Everything I've Ever Wanted to Do

In crafting your vision, we are going to see where your innermost desires are when you don't have time to think. You may be very surprised by what comes up. Today, you are going to **set your timer to five minutes.** You are going to write all of the things down that you want to have.

Revisions: Remove the word "want" and say "I am,"

For example, I am writing a book. I want to write three books, I want to write, start a nonprofit, travel to three islands in a year, etc.

Dream BIGGER than what you thought was possible.

Remember, just because you complete some or all of these items does not mean your life is over and you can roll over and die! It's a jumping-off point; life still continues and it gives you more of a reference on where to go next. You are always going to keep updating your list throughout your life.

Things I Want For Others

It's important to give more than it is to receive. So, for this section, you are going to give double your time and write all of the things that you want for other people. Remember that what you give, you will surely get back. You are writing not to get back but to share with the universe at large that you are ready to give. Remember that you cannot receive with a closed fist. **Set your clock to ten minutes.**

Every single person who pops up into your head, write something that you want for them. Tony Robbins popped up in my head. My concierge person and an old friend. Just feel welcoming to whatever and whoever wants love sent their way.

Each time you feel down, come back to complete this exercise and see what happens.

Craft Your Vision

Now, it's time to make these parts realistic. Review your list and remove the word "want."

Rewrite all of the ways you envision your life by having it.

For example, I *want to* have a monkey. → I have a monkey. I *want to* feel my lover's wet kiss in the morning → I feel my lover's wet kiss.

Part Two

Digging Deeper

Let's go beyond the surface and get to know you and your shiniest points.

You will need space and quiet time.

Inspiring Success

You are here to remember what an inspiring success that you are. Many times, we go beyond ourselves to listen to everyone else for motivation. That changes right now.

You have been through your own hell and back, and if you told people some of the things, their jaw would drop, I'm sure of it.

Today, you are going to share your story of some adversity that you have overcome. Not just to help you get started on your first book or business (although you're welcome), but to remind you of your past and to charge your spirit with the fact that you are an overcomer. When you think about where you have been, you can be ready for where you are going. You are not your past, but it shaped you into the diamond that you are currently.

Feel free to write as many times as you feel called during your progress this year and in the years to come.

Intentions

The Intention is everything. Write the intention behind your vision. It can be something simple or a list.

I.e. The intention behind my vision is to think bigger than what I had been thinking. Or To finish this book no matter what

My intention is:

Future Journal Entry

Today, I am writing about something that I am envisioning. In three years, I am writing my life in extreme and graphic detail.

For example, say you want a relationship. Write in extreme detail about a day in your life. What is a boring day? Is it when you cook food, workout, and do daily tasks like shopping or work in the garden? What type of work do you have? How do you interact? What small disagreements come up? Are you disagreeing with how you should spend the inheritance? One wants to open a nonprofit and the other wants to splurge on another form of business or home improvements. How are you affectionate with one another? What is the air like? How tight was the hug? How wet was the kiss? How amazing was the lovemaking? You get the point; have fun with this.

If you need a time frame for this snapshot exercise, set the timer for 20 minutes.

Candyman, Candyman!

Sometimes, we have to take a long hard look at people in our circle who are not working for us. This is something that requires total honesty. To know that you have a problem, it must be identified.

List people in your life who may be holding you back and write how they are holding you back. Sometimes, it may be that you volunteer to stop yourself from visiting these people. And sometimes, it may be you.

Resolutions! Resolutions! Resolutions!

The good thing is that not all relationships have to be left. Some other ways and strategies can help you move forward in your goals without slamming the door on some of these relationships.

Here are a few tips on how to deal with these people:

People who always shut down anything that you do, you can just not tell them anything. Just smile and accept the simple relationship that it is. If you feel that you can grow and keep this relationship, nourish it.

People who break your spirit: Have a few talks with them.
-Hey, you keep draining my energy when I tell you about things, are you trying to sabotage me?
-Each time I talk about something good, you say very negative things.

For example, when I told you I was surfing, you told me I was a swimmer. I'm not sure whatever I did to you, I deeply apologize. Most of the people around me are not dream crushers, they are supporters. Either you can support me and we can be in contact or this is where the relationship ends.

Sabotagers- Pray to God and ask to reveal the character and motives of people on your team. Friends, colleagues, business associates, and even family members.

Time to Be Of Service to Yourself, Saying Goodbye

The company you keep may be holding you back. When I was in Malibu, California, I met a really sweet guy who wanted to travel longer than he had. He stated out loud that he was feeling like everyone around him wanted to hold him back. "I feel like my friends are trying to break my spirit". When I talked with him again, he was back home and felt like it was a better choice for him.

When you are moving forward, it may be in the best interest to remember two things: "What the enemy meant for evil, God has worked it out for my good." But also, keep in mind that this mantra is not for STAYING in abusive situations. Sometimes, you just need to put on your pants and walk away. You can do it!

So, for today's exercise, I want you to make a list of all of the people who are going to benefit if you are to walk away and make your own way; it may be your future business partner or your children or even your spouse.

Fear in Separation

As you repeat the mantra this morning,

I am not a victim, I'm an overcomer.
I will not be tolerated or beat down, bitter, or chained in hurt.
I am the head and not the tail.
I am unstoppable

When the people you love the most turn out to be those who are stunting your growth, there is a tendency to keep the relationship. This is hurting you at many levels; first, it hurts to be in the relationship and then it hurts to not be yourself. In a way, you are abusing yourself by allowing others to abuse you.

Consider all of the ways you have been in fear, write them down and repeat the same mantra for each person and scenario.

Calling In Your Soulmates

Answering the call of your soul to feel free can be terrifying because it means that things will be done differently.

You will have no more rules that govern your life, just your own principles, ethics, morals, and your own heart. This is highly liberating and there is no book about it, not even a law.

The people around you can help you construct the life you want. As you look deeper into your vision, let's start building a social infrastructure of where you want to be.

Soul Tribe Supporters

These are people who can help you with something you are doing within your vision. Sometimes, they are the people at the co-working space, the housekeeper, or the editor. You can expect all of them to deliver something to you within a deadline. Look at your vision and make a list of all of the people who will support you.

Soul Tribe/ Wolfpack*: Finish liners

In this amazing race towards your vision, there are those people who will be with you through every step of the way, like running a race. There are friends, photographers, and family members who will be there at the finish line waiting to hug you and take photographs of you and with you.

Write a list of all of the people who are benefitting from your journey into your vision. When this is accomplished or while this is happening, these people are benefitting. Create a timetable of how often you will talk to them.

Charlie Gilkey-Start Finishing

Soul Tribe/Wolfpack: Way-showers

The people who have completed certain milestones that you want to achieve are very important to have on this journey because it's lifelong. They will often change, and sometimes, they are not alive. I have had to read many books and watch documentaries to understand some of those for who I want to ask for advice.

Some are alive and your mission is critical to their project and you can connect with them for collaboration. List a few of those way-showers, guides, and mentors who are on the same path and think about the things you will converse with them.

Soul Tribe/ Peers

We all need people whom we can discuss things with, who are on similar boats, right? List those whom you know are also living their dream with their eyes wide open; depending on your dream, this can vary. How often will you talk to them?

Core Values

Your core values are going to drive you to the things you want. These values are principles that you will have while you are living your life with wide open eyes.

The first thing to consider in your core values is the ethics and morals that you have in allowing the vision to live through you. If you are honest and caring, your values will stop you from being with a dishonest partner or taking a corrupt business decision. Let's start there first.

How will you allow your vision to live through you?

Boldly? Passionately? Lightheartedly? Wildly?
You get the point.
I don't want to fill up your head with ideas when you can think for yourself...

First, think of all of the things that you are most passionate about. What would be an issue for which you would fire someone?

Part Three

Removing Blockages: Inner Child Work

Removing Blockages: Everyone has an inner child. Sometimes, when moving forward, we tend to self-sabotage. Today, you are going to write with your least dominant hand and ask your inner child to write a love letter to you.

Being a Good Parent to Your Inner Child

Everyone has an inner child. Sometimes, when moving forward, we tend to self-sabotage. Today, you are going to write with your least dominant hand and ask your inner child to write a list of all of the things he or she wants. To move forward in life and work together with all parts of you, a union must happen. Make sure that your vision includes things and ways that your inner child needs to feel good.

Resolving Your Past

Everyone has an inner child. Sometimes, when moving forward, we tend to self-sabotage. Today, you are going to write with your least dominant hand and ask your inner child to tell his or her story. What happened and what does he or she need from you? (This exercise may take some time, but dedicate yourself to finishing it; you are already winning).

Cartoon time!

Today, you are going to bring that creative energy back out. Create a comic strip of a problem in your life and make the most AMAZING, outrageous, and funny solution you could imagine.

Often, the problem is bigger in our heads than in reality. Today, you are going to create your own reality. Have fun and think out of the box. Feel free to do this when you get stuck in a rut, lighten the mood, and remind yourself there are so many other possibilities.

Part Four

Taking Action

You have done so much work on yourself, and now, it's time to take action on your vision.

"Remember, the difference between you and the person you envy is that you settled for less". Dr. Phil

Getting real!

Set up a list for yourself.

- Social Life
- Living
- Dating/ Romance
- Financially
- Investments
- Sexually (with your husband or wife)
- Physically
- Spiritually
- Taking action
- Giving back
- Self-growth
- Family

Be REAL. Write all of the things that went well and what you like about this area of life.

Getting real!

Set up a list for yourself.

- Social Life
- Living /Housing

- Dating/ Romance
- Financially
- Investments
- Sexually (with your husband or wife)
- Physically
- Spiritually
- Taking action
- Giving back
- Self-growth
- Family

Get REAL. Write all of the things that needed more work and what you are going to do about it to get to where you want.

Be Your Own Best Friend Today

Today's journal entry is writing a letter of advice to yourself as if you are your own best friend.

Whatever circumstance you need help in, before looking for a therapist or life coach, search within yourself. Explain what the problem is and with empowering words, accept your own advice. This helps tremendously when accepting your

In my letter to myself, I needed to write a letter proving that I needed to continue listening to myself. I wrote that no one in the universe had my set of fingerprints and it is important not to follow anyone.

Read your letter out loud and follow your advice **today**.

Failure!

Let's talk about failure for a moment. There is a motivational speech I listen to about falling forward by Denzel Washington. He is amazing and talks about getting rid of the backup plan and says that there is no such thing. The backup plan means that you are not dedicated to your plan.

As long as you fall forward, you are going to give everything, all that you have. Ditch the backup plan.

For example, if you have plans to move out of town, create different scenarios:

Action plan: *Go to the world's largest and free university, youtube.com and search Fall Forward by Denzel Washington. Next, create an action plan for falling forward.*

Reminder to keep revising

As you are reviewing all of the works that you have done. It's important to keep in touch with your vision.

Keep writing all about the exciting days in your future journal. Keep writing about the boring days and now that you are taking action, it's time to ask for divine intervention.

Making Space by Clearing the Time

As you consider all of the things that you need to do, break all of your time up into four blocks of time.

Administrative time - you can answer emails and run errands.

Social time - talking and meeting with people in your wolf pack.

Focus time - requires ALL of you, your energy, focus, and this is where the world CANNOT reach you.

Rest and relaxation - you may need to work out, take naps, socialize, meditate, whatever gets you back in your space of fire.

With your vision, you will find that you have several projects at once and this is extremely helpful in building your days, months, quarterly and yearly goals.

List all of the things that you have left to do this year/month/week in order to feel complete.

Vision Board Time!!

Picture yourself in your new life:

For this activity, you will need lots of images of yourself. This will take several days and even weeks to collect physical representations of what you will have in your life.

Do the same for a body type or activity. For example, if you want to be better at boxing, cut out an image and place yourself there. Do this for all of the lists where you were honest with yourself and all of the things that you wish to do, have, and experience.

Take a few blank checks and write checks out for yourself in various amounts.

Help yourself to understand that this is real you can use a notebook or canva.com. I recommend both.

Routine:

As someone who nomads, routines have not exactly been easy. I've found an amazing purpose in creating a formula for the morning and evening.

For the morning, write a list of all of the things that you would do in a day if you had plenty of time in the day. (It really helps if you write all of the things that make you feel good) I will list a few but by now, you understand that I prefer you to think for yourself.

-Workout
-swim
-pray
-prepare meals for the week on Friday

Morning Routines:

Charlie Gilkey recommends a few things from his book *Start Finishing*. I enjoyed this book; in fact, I take it to every place I travel. For this, I recommend following his advice. To review what you've done the night before and prepare for the day.

Where did you leave off in your work? What are you looking forward to today? What routine in this morning is going to show that you are disciplined?

Grow Your Spirit!

Fasting is one of the most powerful tools used in all philosophies throughout the world. When I lived in Thailand, for vipassana meditation, we would eat only in the morning at 6 and then at 9, nothing after that.

In Malaysia, I had the pleasure of traveling during Ramadan and the fast was no food or drinks until sundown.

In Christianity and a previous book, I wrote about going through three days deliverance fast of water only. Today, to uplift your spirit, you are going to fast for the entire day until dinner, focusing on whatever it is that you want. Why? Fasting speeds everything up and is a total game changer!

-To reveal the motives of people around you.
- For guidance on moving forward on a business decision.
-To speed up something that is already coming- accelerated promotion, deliverance, unlimited success.

Advanced: Continue your fast for 21 days eating only vegan food. All forms of fruits and vegetables, tofu and grains. No additional salt, milk, yogurt, cream, eggs, or animals. You can do it!

Ad

Money, Multiple Streams of Income, and Investments

Today and through this week as you review your list of improvements, I'd like you to get on the world's best and free university YouTube and do research on types of investments. Pick two to move forward with. Remember that this is a vow to live frugally and **be** wealthy, not look wealthy .

-Real estate

-Stocks/ bonds/ Exchange Traded Funds

-Gold and silver bullion

-Crypto currency

-Ecommerce

-creating online courses/YouTube channel

-Infinite Banking

-Overseas investments

-Publishing books

Your Strangest Secret

Earl Nightingale is one of my favorite speakers. He talks about creating a 30-day test. Take a note card and write the one thing you want. Don't think about how it will happen, but approach it with a cheerful attitude and to leave all the rest up to the powers unknown. Do this for your vision. Make it clear and plain.
YouTube **"The Strangest Secret".**

On the back, write the words from the Sermon on the Mount: Ask, and it will be given to you; search, and you will find; knock and the door will be opened for you. For everyone who asks receives and everyone who searches finds, and for everyone who knocks, the door will be opened."

Begin the test while you are working through this book.

You did it!

Do a little dance, play some awesome music, get a massage. You can keep calm now; your life has an ultimate direction! Congrats on making it to the end of this workbook. It was a lot of work, but you rocked it **so** hard. Give yourself a really long hug. Like a REALLY long hug. You broke a few generational curses, made a new list of friends and supporters, learned about yourself, grew in your finances, and created an action plan on building your new reality. This is just the beginning. No one else has the stories that you have in your perspective and the dreams you share. There is a reason you are here to complete the divine expression and that is "YOU". There is nothing left to prove, it is already done. Just do it. God bless you!

Please leave a review on Amazon and our socials to help the mission of helping others. Thank you so much!

Unapologetically,
Morenike

www.ingramcontent.com/pod-product-compliance
Lightning Source LLC
Chambersburg PA
CBHW031506040426
42444CB00007B/1221